Memory Marries Desire

poems by

Gary Glauber

Finishing Line Press
Georgetown, Kentucky

Memory Marries Desire

Copyright © 2016 by Gary Glauber
ISBN 978-1-944899-21-9 First Edition
All rights reserved under International and Pan-American Copyright Conventions.
No part of this book may be reproduced in any manner whatsoever without written permission from the publisher, except in the case of brief quotations embodied in critical articles and reviews.

ACKNOWLEDGMENTS

Many thanks to the kind editors of the following journals in which these poems first appeared:

Blue Heron Review: "Rivulets and Tributaries"
The Blue Hour Magazine: "Talisman"
Brickplight: "Reliquary"
Calliope Magazine: "Celebrated Mirage," "Inception"
Fade Poetry Journal: "Aftermath"
Fine Flu Journal: "Rumors Fly"
Foliate Oak Literary Journal: "Small World"
The Gambler Magazine: "Raucous Summer Sunset," "Old Timer"
Indian Summer Quarterly: "The Gray Life"
The Legendary: "The Second Breakfast," "Translation," "Succession"
Silver Birch Press: "Inner Echo"
Stone Path Review: "Capsized"
Twisted Vine Literary Arts Journal: "The Next Table"
Verse-Virtual: "The Other"
Xenith: "No Relation"

Editor: Christen Kincaid
Cover Photo: Gary Glauber
Author Photo: Zane Glauber
Cover Design: Elizabeth Maines

Printed in the USA on acid-free paper.
Order online: www.finishinglinepress.com
            also available on amazon.com

Author inquiries and mail orders:
Finishing Line Press
P. O. Box 1626
Georgetown, Kentucky 40324
U. S. A.

Table of Contents

Translation 1
The Next Table 3
Rivulets and Tributaries 4
The Other 5
Inner Echo 7
Aftermath 9
Raucous Summer Sunset 10
Tango 11
Origin of the Specious 12
Small World 14
No Relation 15
Inception 16
Capsized 17
Black Oak Credenza 18
Talisman 19
Succession 20
Conductivity 21
Rumors Fly 23
Assailed By Reality 24
Reliquary 25
The Second Breakfast 26
Transcendence 28
Old Timer 29
Celebrated Mirage 31
The Gray Life 32
Scenario 33

A poet is an unhappy being whose heart is torn by secret sufferings, but whose lips are so strangely formed that when the sighs and the cries escape them, they sound like beautiful music...and then people crowd about the poet and say to him: "Sing for us soon again;" that is as much as to say, "May new sufferings torment your soul."

~Soren Kierkegaard, *Either/Or*

Translation

A madman mumbles in the shadows
as the corner of your eye catches
the woman across the way,
smiling shyly, perhaps sympathetic
to the situation's awkwardness.
The world boasts a bounty of secrets and rust,
and we race the clock's circles.

You grab his hand, like a child,
the man who once stood so proud,
and now there's nothing behind vacant eyes.
He looks at the restaurant window,
sees nothing, a wounded crab
scuttling across sidewalks
that might as well be ocean floor.
His other hand grips hard
the cane that seems to lead him forward.

It is a dark time of year,
even the moon is off hiding.
The vacant lot is a seat of dangers,
a forbidden place to avoid,
glass shards and impending injury,
a feeble excuse for geography.

The wind blows order from its place.
You smooth hair back with memories
of younger days, equinoxes and convergences,
the pungent aroma of father's cologne.
The night air is rich with redolence,
circuitous crosses and turns
that stir the dust of reminiscence.

You recall the smell,
your mother's cigarettes,
the clink of cocktail glasses,
the mirrored tray of cut glass bottles
and magical powders and balms.

Still, the night refuses to leave.
It is a number on the door.
You climb into the strangely reticent bed
and suddenly the madman's mumbles
begin to make sense:
sleep brings on life lessons.

The Next Table

Death is the current running wild
through black rivers of conversation;
all those respective creatures toppled
in battles to parade onward past time.

Gossip of daisies pushing up through
body remnants, clutching at sunlight
through limbs, signets of vacant dreams,
a past world's luxuries and lusts.

Dark mascara underlines eyes
that experience such survivor's glee,
unsettled victors in expensive prints
celebrating the avoidance of anguish.

Nostalgia is a privilege of existence,
and their simmering murmurs bubble
with a subtle soupcon of charmed concern,
hushed as white noise on the horizon.

A flash emits unfettered abstract joy
but this triumph is ephemeral, empty,
and none of these canny diners can predict
whose reservations will next go unheld.

Rivulets and Tributaries

The unnamed waterways of bygone youth:
that winding iced-over stream of secret winter sledding
dangerous and fast, cold and delicious,
the snaking rill behind the brook park where bullfrogs croaked,
even the small wooded creek, once mysterious and imposing,
now all fade to rusty memory, whole neighborhoods,
landmarks reduced to hearsay and rumination.
Immeasurable gallons traversed these anonymous circuits,
and now streams of consciousness flow back
throwing sounds and smells upon themselves.
The tiny animals, local rocks and flora, merge
with names and community waterholes:
Joe's luncheonette, Herb's candy store,
the bakery on a weekend morning,
where natures of other types were delved and explored.
Somewhere in the world scientists dig,
hoping to unearth artifacts, shed light on darkness,
analyze and synthesize to best explain the past.
I do the same, wandering this pine forest,
extracting torrents of memory from
rivers one generation nearly explored,
soon lost to the rolling delta of time.

The Other

They all looked so clean cut:
sharp angles, healthy curves, fine features,
chiseled to an All-American profile.
They presented variations on a theme,
handsome boys who played trombone,
fetching girls who danced quite seriously,
each successive one in their many numbers
slightly different from respective predecessor.
They stood up proudly for each other,
as if a team, an army, a legion of sorts.
You could see them in attendance
at plays and band recitals, taking up
whole rows in the school auditorium,
watching performing brothers and sisters,
stately grandparents mixed in with
older and younger brethren,
rooting as one for the filial cause.
My dysfunctional family could not have
been more disparate:
small, bickering, miserable,
raising argument to an art form.
Maybe that explains my love and envy,
watching those pretty faces
devoted to watching kith and kin,
wearing secret smiles, an inner society
which I could never hope to join.
While my heart realized
no family could manage
such an aura of perfect paradise,
they seemed to master the illusion.
I studied them before the lights went down
and during lengthy intermissions,

longing in dreams to be accepted
as one of their brethren band,
sitting in those long rows,
one of the beautiful family.

Inner Echo

We grew up in that buffer
twixt city and suburb,
next to a busy thruway.
Our landmark
was the racetrack,
built at one century's end,
whose grandstand's outer walls stood
green and visible from everywhere,
whose large digital clock revealed
numbers of how late or early
one's return trip home actually was.

Harness racing lived there,
a foreign separate world existing
right beside our own,
small drivers wearing striped silks
sitting in two-wheeled sulkies,
eight races nightly.

It was a familiar background ritual,
thousands roaring with bets on the line,
urging on chosen horses and drivers,
stirring up dirt on that half-mile oval.
You could hear excitement as you drove by,
catch glimpses of trotters in motion,
bright fluorescents illuminating action
as summer skies faded from blue to black
like some disparate Magritte landscape.

Whenever a horse lacked hustle
sufficient to a driver's desire,
out would come the light whip
to motivate the animal with noise
by striking the sulky's shaft.
Strict rules governed

the usage of such whips,
but enthused racing fanatics
would shout it loud, clear, and often:
"Go to the whip, Hervé!"

I'm not sure how the term transferred
to our schoolboy vernacular,
but it did, forever lodged
in heads and hearts, an anthem
urging better selves to strive harder.
During that tough calculus test,
during football practice,
even on that hot romantic weekend date,
that crowd voice in our brains,
motivating us to go ever harder,
do it far faster, strike us on
to ultimate victory.

It became our catchphrase,
soon adopted by those without
the slightest inkling of
its harness racing origin.

Now we've all grown up,
moved to places more remote.
Raceway has become redesigned casino,
the large clock gone,
harness racing a mere afterthought.
Still, whenever I dig deep down
for an ounce of extra motivation,
I hear the familiar phrase
that sets me on to achieve
because, in the final estimation,
you never leave your hometown.

Aftermath

Your silhouette whispers
from the bunker of darkened bedsheets
as if there was no blame attached
to these clandestine gatherings.
And yet you maintain it's only business,
an aspect of the larger whole,
an accidental adjunct like smoke from a fire,
something that dissipates in the air over time,
wisps of thought disappearing
as if the heart could avoid attachments.
Strangely,
painfully,
you believe it.

Raucous Summer Sunset

The mood swings, pumps legs to go higher,
seeking kindred sufferers in a linear progression.
Yet the mist prevents such progress, and
all intention is reflected in the still waters,
the overripe temptation and naked possibility,
gifts from her father along with his scorn.
The sky explodes with color, brooding
and preserving memory, absentmindedly.
Scattered details fade with the light,
as clouds that hold answers swiftly disappear
in the gall of corrupted nightfall.

Tango

A veritable chorus kicks up inside my heart,
announcing a familiar narrative, easy prey
to the graceful in alluring dishabille or no,
attuned to the movement, the rhythm driving
the sway and rustle, the exposed ease of such fluidity.
I am tenderly ensnared, mesmerized for the moment.

Having touched the soft skin encasing those muscles,
the sweet ligature binding the whole package together,
I feel this map of unexpected power, softly guiding
torso forward, testament to practiced self-control,
hours of long training to make such elegance second nature,
transcendent beauty wherein dance tells silent story.

I stare at the body, glistening in light, dynamic even at rest.
Anticipation is confidence transforming to energy,
making connections, articulation as larger message,
shared and fixed like a butterfly pinioned in place,
then set free to fly again, fluttering in sweet resurrection,
unexpected and delightful. I stop to smile, then applaud.

Later bodies converge in fixed choreography
of latent desire and need, traversing corners
and sampling angles without hesitancy or reservation,
executing nature's orders, the mute magnificence of
entwined musculature, the heat of improvised performance.
Clichés are uttered and ignored, eyes exchange promises.

Victim to interpretation again, reading murky shadows
on dim bedroom walls, hieroglyphs of a strange culture,
convoluted and deconstructed into fortunes and bonhomie.
I let my brain trail behind, dusty thoughts trying to keep pace
with quickened heartbeats and the feeling of sated exhaustion
masquerading as some grand agile accomplishment.

Origin of the Specious

It was ours
in the way secrets discovered
allow entry into a private club:
illicit lovers revealed,
confirming months of rumors
as they waited for his divorce
to finalize.

Tall Larry from Marketing,
mild-mannered in appearance,
was surprisingly more than meek.
Short-haired Jessica from Research
apparently checked him out thoroughly
and liked what she found.

They'd been spotted in restaurants
and local bars, smiling their way
through awkward "coincidences."
Many thought her young enough
to be his daughter,
but that might be a stretch.
The age difference was there,
but what of it?
Love is a strange thing
often resisting explanation
even to those in the throes of it.

The talk breathed life into our
pale gray carpeted cubicles,
providing shiny new talking points
for those seeking vicarious thrills.
We were grateful for the distraction,
for soon enough it'll be back
to humdrum routines
of mundane existence,
sending out feelers to confirm
the next juicy bit of office gossip.

Small World

We were at the Floridian,
enthusiastic kids in tow,
hoping the buddy system
might assist us through
the heat wave, the long lines,
and the next gift shop.

We were in another world,
dreaming of international espionage,
not just negotiating a character breakfast,
but the fate of all humankind:
importance, relevance, esprit de corps.

We were monitored round the clock.
Paying far too much for way too little,
yet slowly eroding, caving in
to the overseer's relentless wishes,
seeing eye-to-eye in a friendly corporate way.

Buying those mouse ears
seemed a good idea at the time,
but a week later,
skin itchy and tan fading,
contentiously ensconced
back in the cubicle's tenuous solitude,
menial obligations and spreadsheets galore,
we open our eyes as if emerging from a coma,
and wonder, "What were we thinking?"

No Relation

No relation, she says, tossing off an assumption
that years and travels would lead to ample coverage
of names. But the reputation feels ill-gotten, now that time
has intervened as a buffer between that world of long ago
and now. The past is some cloudy other, a fiction,
a parable of once was and spritely youth, innocence lost
back when reasons mattered less and simplicity danced for free.
For a moment, he is lost in the throes of a sweet reverie,
but the clamor of some dropped tray in the pub's kitchen
brings him back in a hurry. She is working two jobs,
seeking to save up and furnish the new place she moved to
since breaking up with that guy, the unsteady steady,
he who promised without delivering, year after expectant year.
It has been difficult, she relates, approaching holidays alone,
doing things with friends that knew her only as half of a couple.
The dichotomy is strangest at large parties and occasions,
when it seems sides are chosen, allegiances pledged, and
fresh awkwardness encountered. She expresses a desire
to escape it all, to travel to China for a month next summer,
to traverse those same Silk Roads that inform her lessons
while building history of her own. Everyone has such
exotic stories, she says, yet she remains hesitant,
unsure as a teetering economy, worried about job security
and the notion of being so far away, so long. He encourages her
to risk it, knowing the mad genius of youth is best realized
through the freedom of uncertainty and possible peril.
Now is your time, and there's much to be gained,
he reminds her, remembering when he too could throw
caution to the wind and chase rainbows to foreign horizons.

Inception

Swelling buds
burst into blossom,
fomenting as though forged
from God's own cauldron.
So much hidden here
amongst woods
flushed with flower:
sow thistle and sneezeweed,
succulent saplings
sheltering flame
in unfurled stalks
like fingers off small angry fists.
A holy wave of silence spreads
as earth turns egg, impregnated
by a rustling rutting wind,
awaiting future delivery of
a someday sun-kissed harvest
of pulse and possible progress.

Capsized

Winter stole the river's primal significance,
but his duty remained to note what drifted by.
Smokestacks abandoned upstream were
his silent accomplices: watching, waiting.

In the semi-still waters, he could
see his reflection, hair silvering
on the edges, like his father before him.
Those same intense eyes burned
whenever told what to do directly,
but now the fire smoldered less.

The end of his youth was floating
in front of his eyes, dreams carried
by weak current into the swirling eddy
that might be the rest of his life.

The lone spectator contemplated
this river of his ancestors, and skipped stones
to escape hard lessons before him.

Black Oak Credenza

Between sobs, she haltingly provides three reasons.
It's interesting how none coincide with his three reasons.

Their silence is punctuated by expired electronic timers
that serve to remind of lovemaking for three reasons.

The ice-covered branches are forks of the gods
that are waved in angry anticipation of three reasons.

The coffee-table magazine offers fifty important tips,
but none approach the secret revelation of three reasons.

He dreams other dreams of velvety softness, familiar laughter,
while breathing, smiling in sleep, heeding three reasons.

She sells all his furniture except for this one piece
where she stores intimate secrets of the three reasons.

She holds the key, a secret drawer storing poisons created,
reminding of shared recipes and a bounty of three reasons.

Yet she throws him out, leaves *G-Money* to wrong-headed devices.
Scolded, he suffers toward supplication: pleas three reasons.

Talisman

I am in back of the classroom pretending,
thrilled that none read my mind, elsewhere,
pondering a world beyond this page's penguins,
the secrets hiding behind my pretty classmate's skirt.
She smiles to tell me I will never find out either.
Now, astride this cold tent in the barren wild,
I am drawn to this past, the simplicity of life then,
glistening caves where the cold was tolerable, sustainable,
unlike the sub-zero dangers surrounding, confounding me.
Encaged within hard walls of thought, I alone
review the progression that has comprised this journey,
while a reaper in the distance calls my name within
the dark chorus of the wolves' hungry howls
and I pray to the forces that might beget mercy,
speaking languages unknown and universal,
eyes shut and body shivering, reminded of
the apocryphal sacrifices meant to teach us
obscure lessons of comfort and unlikely hope.

Succession

A thimbleful of air,
shaken onto that morning sleeping face,
like mist crawling over mystery swamp.
He inhales the sweet tang, an aroma
of hope, odor of efficiency, of technical
prowess pegged into a modern world,
all things in their uniformed place.
No starched collars reveal crimson lip stains,
no yellow passions aching honest pretenders.
He focuses on daily chores,
rituals of habit performed with steadfast care,
buttons pressed and levers pulled,
a panoply of complex maneuvers negotiated.
She was adopted once, plucked from
the anonymous horde, fashioned to be
the angel whose affections might redeem him.
She never did, through no fault of her own.
Now villagers with pitchforks and torches
voice their discontent with what they perceive
to be injustice, an attack of malfeasance,
a mad wind from the polar north.
She remains loyal, even though his restless mind
is distracted by zealous fictions.
He puts on armor and sallies forth,
recanting exotic tales of yesteryear,
legerdemain and legend, ferocity's histrionics,
but in the light of day, few take note
and already another is appointed;
the kingdom has moved on.

Conductivity

The recital hall crowds with expectation;
hushed silence as shared heartbeat.
Cog in the orchestral wheel, he prepares to roll,
traversing each careful note to confidently
convey the composer's original intention.
White shirt starched to crisp attention
provides necessary camouflage
to achieve strategic means.

She walks front and center
through heavy applause,
formal black gown elegant and suggestive,
opaque on smooth shoulders.
She comes to tame the pressure,
to harness and guide intensity into art.
Her beauty strikes him yet again,
tempered by years, but still viable.
This former actress remains
calm under duress as maestro,
smiling while wielding the thin baton,
as intimate with the piece
as if she had penned it herself.

She summons orchestra to readiness,
bows raised, breaths taken awaiting
her signal to launch the volley of notes
that starts this musical journey.
Like a Von Karajan or Toscanini,
she manages a distinctive individuality,
gestures carrying the music that carries her,
a reciprocal arrangement culling
notes to life through performance.

He is servant to her master's wand;
required phrasings and accents
coaxed from seasoned professionals
with sweeps of the arm, a well-timed glare,
one he likes to pretend is meant
for him as her favorite.

Yet he is a bit player,
no chances for a star turn,
retained month-to-month 'til the contracted one
returns from maternity leave.
Playing his heart out, following the spirit
of each score to his best abilities,
dreaming that this maestro's smooth legato
might someday summon a romantic sweep
of rising strings from within, a love shared
beyond performance, beyond the
love of music that unites them now.

Rumors Fly

Our silence splinters
with the staccato breath
of hyper histrionics.
I dissolve into your
imagined tirade,
knowing no rules
in this played non-game.
Ignoring danger,
making love
to your heart alone.

Cannot feign ignorance
or undo all that's done,
cannot unsee this tragedy shared
or untangle our complex past.

It's become our mythology,
believed by all the locals,
translated loosely from the
hieroglyphs of nuance,
repeated gestures made
in the express checkout line.

We check the mailbox
three times in short succession,
continue to wait for news
that's never coming.
Butterflies mock us,
but in the end,
we fight imaginary battles alone.

Assailed By Reality

The overarching beauty and horror *is* the point,
but they watch the change of season on screens,
text lunch orders, tweet shallow reflections,
take pride in their distance from nature's harsh glare.

As the creator toys about with the devil's tithing,
I list for them grotesqueries of the parasites,
how the feeding stylops turn insects intersex,
how the eye-moths feed on blood, pus, and tears.

The emphasis need be on what is, for the past
becomes less predictor of present dilemmas,
and the yearly groupings go mute in their timidity,
afraid to assume a misguided stance, fearing repercussion.

She reminds that the world festers in suppurating sores,
old and broken past mending, frayed and nibbled at the edges.
This lover of solitude, so able to capture in resplendent language
the childlike wonder at small daily miracles, asks difficult questions.

She expects no answers, and continues to explore anew,
each day an opportunity for lessons in living and learning.
I exert energy in executing enthusiastic efforts,
but the words ring in an echo of virtual classroom silence
and I too find myself breathing alone in the dark.

Reliquary

He and the young waitress
share a sweet smile as she passes.
At this age, he reads nothing into it,
letting such potential betrayals
find other more willing participants.
With certitude, he knows plenty yet
are lured by the throes of emotive drama,
unknowable ways of the human heart,
smooth like sea glass only after
rough business of thousands of waves
have worked their tortured polishing act
overnight, over seasons and years.
The gray at his temples
is earned much the same way.
Let it serve as visual reminder,
warning and testament,
a ruffed collar that indicates
a very different age.

The Second Breakfast

The second breakfast was not lavish.
It was conciliatory; eaten alone,
clouded with heavy thoughts,
strong espresso, and long reflection.

He pondered the impossibility
of making it work.

She was kind, sweet,
attentive, interested.
She approached, a smiling stranger,
asking, "Have any plans for breakfast?"

The maneuver's playful candor
subtly insinuated her into his life.
He admired the forwardness,
let himself be charmed into the invite.

The night proved pleasant enough;
morning delivered the promise
of superb banana-chocolate chip pancakes,
then she left.

Now, he was eating again, but less.
The second breakfast was a time for decisions.

She was older, a former French major,
a little exotic, a nurse with varied shifts.
Beyond that, she hadn't told him much:
she lived in town, enjoyed the pancakes.

Hesitant, he wasn't sold
on another steady relationship
so close on the heels
of last year's crash and burn.

Over a bite of toast, he searched
for graceful ways out, pouring another cup,
debating compassion, morals, obligations,
sip by painful sip.

Transcendence

Watching the bird that does not wish to be seen,
it kisses the water's surface in strange charade—
three-word movie title, something about nature,
but I'm having none of it.
Lay your eggs before me,
I remain loyal to my pledge,
invisible spectator,
outsider to this dimpled oblivion,
gathering up concentric ripples,
distributing them purposefully
in random and ordinary ways.
I yell at the bees in Latin,
flush the locusts from the weeds,
curse the mighty force controlling us.
The light comes on suddenly,
consciousness floating on its back,
betrayed by stalking its beauty,
diminutive and real,
a moment captured even now,
genuflecting and genuine,
waiting ever so quietly
for evolution's slow change.

Old Timer

The road calls you home,
serpentine, unspectacular,
nestling close to the lake
before blossoming into
asphalt cloverleaf.
Hidden from the elements,
your brain's GPS sends silent directives
as you motor along, intent on heading
one way and then another,
on a mission to return and wonder,
what became of her, the large family,
late days of relatives and sweet sunset views.

Now winter waves its frozen wand,
turning leaves to dusty memories,
leaving trunks of anxious skeletons
pontificating wildly in the nether wind.

That summer the serial killer
unleashed the panic,
she and you parked in the lot
below the nursing home,
too lazy to go picnic,
content with groping in the car.

Today a continent divides you
from an empty house beside
the culvert out past the dead end road.

And the world finds new anxieties.

Children drive down their own roads,
thinking new thoughts that you also had
nearly a generation ago, when debauchery
was almost allowable, a calculated chance
any young one might dare take.

Swore you'd never go back,
cursed the world in a heap of hurt anger,
but time removes and absolves you,
soothes you into forgiveness
too long after the fact.
You put the blinker on
and turn.

Celebrated Mirage

The holiday is pointless, the party even more so.
Everyone eats, drinks, watches the clock,
mingling a slow waltz between
well-decorated rooms bursting
with knick knacks and family photos,
not a table or mantelpiece vacant.
Groups are gathered by the glue of small talk,
local politics, the threat of coyotes to small pets,
but mostly reflections on the year and younger years,
running outside at midnight with eager enthusiasm,
disappointed by the lack of hovercrafts and monorails.
Now the hostess' BFF is flirting with me in the kitchen,
and I should be flattered, this well put together woman
in an elegant black party dress is trying to feed me
someone's ambitious online idea for a savory canapé.
Another me might have found the gesture inviting,
but this year's me is grumpy and mildly annoyed,
wishing for louder music, pulse and electricity
to stir other senses, power me past the tired list
of resolutions, more this, less that, and all the other.
I see an older version of a former college acquaintance.
He is taller and balder than remembered.
He once held the heart of a girl I madly desired;
I envied the magic he managed then.
Now he introduces me to his new wife
and silently I am glad to be unimpressed.
Time marches on, and when the clock hands
come together at the top and middle,
I go through the polite motions,
kissing cheeks, shaking hands,
the same old pretender from seconds ago,
way back in the old year.

The Gray Life

The stunted realization
opened like a thirsty blossom,
like a string of days filled
with restless surcease,
anger to denial to acceptance.
A question of relevancy,
of relation in matters of time,
an inevitable transformation
of generational replacement,
a verity of survival versus
the fickle ways of the human heart.
What's left is isolation,
the music stopped and one chair less,
a world no longer welcoming,
a way outlasted, a purpose
withdrawn like a truant entertainer,
one act too late.

Scenario

In the dream, I am part of some erstwhile crime investigation unit. I am the older, craggy one, the wizened veteran who has seen better days. Younger, more handsome and ravishingly beautiful assistants surround me, most of whom are only capable of iterating inane comments. "They don't get any deader than that," says the attractive heartthrob to my left, some Jason or Jared or Justin or Jeremy. I give him my best glare. "Why would anyone kill a dancer?" says the fair-haired rookie to my right. "Isn't that obvious?" queries the fetching blonde woman who seems young enough to be someone's granddaughter. "She used to be a hairstylist." Her conviction is astounding, as if a bad dye job might easily justify a murder. I give them my best exasperated grunt, signifying the tolerance needed to get me through to the next scene, when we're flying back to some high tech lab hidden in some remote snow-capped mountainside. I am being served ginger ale, and the flight attendants look like they all could be my assistants. "Looks like a bad week for foreign interests," says the man across from me, apropos of nothing, and then he looks up eagerly, as if awaiting a response. I have no knowledge of any sort that could shed light on this situation. In fact, I am wondering about the files in front of me, a hefty pile of potential suspects. Each folder contains a picture or two, usually a domestic scene, a posed smile, a casual encounter for said evildoer. Beneath this, a series of questions and replies, as if each individual had been the subject of some bizarre centerfold interview in a magazine circulated only to intelligence agents with a high level of clearance. Pet peeves? Cannibals and airport gate attendants. Favorite color? Blue. We land and I soon meet up with Mr. Kingport, our R&D expert. He shows me a short video that seems to be about the uncanny rotation of the major league knuckleball. I am not piecing any of this together, and he seems impatient with my confusion. "We only have six hours," he says, "and then the locals will be stepping all over this." I nod, and grab a handful of the gizmos and gadgets he stores in a large basket near what always struck me as a gift shop next door. These dreams never have commercial interruptions, although if they did, I am certain that it would be younger versions of me driving the cars and doing the necessary manual labor to sell the wares to keep the show on the air. On the plane ride back to our offices, the foreign interests guy asks about my progress on the case. "Almost there," I assure him, and he seems content with that. He tells me that the coroner's report revealed some surprises, and I wonder if he is someone I should know after all. I review that report, and it turns out that all the serial murders could be connected easily through a college club for technical innovation, a geek society that our own Kingport had belonged to back in the day. Our killer was a man incensed by several stolen patents, seeking revenge. As usual, my announcement of this seems to take everyone by surprise. They clap me on the back, and send the boys in blue off to bring him to eventual justice. The pretty assistant girl smiles at me, and seems glad that this was solved before it might affect her weekend's social plans. "Sometimes the simple things are so incredibly complex," says the kid with the J-name, and the rookie expresses agreement and amazement, as if this is a profound proclamation. I button up my coat against the wind, preparing for my next adventure, or the next workday, whichever comes first.

Gary Glauber is a poet, fiction writer, and teacher. This past April, to celebrate National Poetry Month, he took part in *Found Poetry Review*'s PoMoSco project. Two years prior, he was part of the *Pulitzer Remix* project. He has had poems and short stories published in numerous venues, both online and in print. His work has been nominated for the *Pushcart Prize* and *Best of the Net*. He is a champion of the underdog who often composes to an obscure power pop soundtrack. His first full-length collection, *Small Consolations* (Aldrich Press), is available from Amazon.com.

www.ingramcontent.com/pod-product-compliance
Lightning Source LLC
Chambersburg PA
CBHW060224050426
42446CB00013B/3158